CRAFTING A DAILY PRACTICE

A SIMPLE COURSE ON SELF-COMMITMENT

T. THORN COYLE

Copyright © 2017 / 2022
T. Thorn Coyle
PF Publishing

Cover Art and Design © 2022
Thorn Coyle

Editing:
Dayle Dermatis

Paperback ISBN: 978-1-946476-44-9

A shorter paperback version of this book was originally published in April, 2012 by Sunna Press under the ISBN 9780692992203

WHY DAILY PRACTICE?

Daily practice supports our lives.
Daily practice helps us to know ourselves better.

Daily practice enables us to return to center more quickly.

Daily practice becomes the foundation upon which we build our lives.

By connecting us to ourselves, daily practice also connects us to the world outside. This helps us cultivate lives of greater clarity and service.

The dailiness of it is primary. Too often we rush into our days, scattered and fragmented, or conversely, we may start our days feeling sluggish and ill, with no support to help us feel better. As both a person who has off and on struggled with chronic illness and, for a period, chronic pain, and as someone who is ambitious and driven, I've experienced a whole range within this spectrum.

And I know that finally committing to regular daily spiritual practice helped my life more than any other thing. Daily practice gave me inner structure and consistency. It held up a mirror and showed me myself, in all my parts. Daily practice reflected my bravery, my pettiness, my weakness, my strength, my sorrow, and my desire.

By learning to sit with myself, I learned to notice more, to not fall prey to every passing thought or emotion, and to not fall prey to outside forces, either. My life, even in the midst of turmoil, remained much more steady than it could otherwise be.

And it was the daily return to the center of myself—and to my relationships with my ancestors, my deities, and the space around me—that gave me the steady tiller by which to steer my life.

I'm not saying that I always act with grace. Messiness still happens. Mistakes are still made. But once my practice was firmly established, getting trapped in counterproductive patterns lessened, and sometimes even ceased. I can see the patterns now, and while they might grip me for a short time, they do not stay.

Because every morning, I align my soul. I breathe. I pray. I make offerings. I sit with myself. And then I begin the remainder of my day.

Daily practice sets a template for what follows. Also, engaging in daily practice, no matter how small, reminds all of the parts of ourselves that we matter.

We are worth showing up for.

Throughout this course, we'll talk more about

adjusting practices for our particular lives, conditions, and abilities, or how our practice itself may wax and wane. But right now, I want us to breathe in the possibility that we can commit to ourselves, our lives, our minds, bodies, and souls.

We can forge a sacred compact to hold our own hands, and to seek out help when help is needed.

FEAR AND PRACTICE

"The state of emancipation toward which we are journeying is freedom from the fear of loss."
—Kabir Helminsky

We so much fear losing things: relationships, money, our good names, children, jobs...but most often, what we most fear losing are parts of ourselves. Every time an angel appears in any story, the first words they speak are, "Be not afraid." I think they say that, not only to assure the person in question that the angels won't hurt them, but also as an acknowledgment that big changes will be coming. Those big changes usually entail loss. Courage will be required.

While teaching a class on daily practice, I developed a hunch that we often avoid daily practice not out of laziness, or lack of discipline, but because we know that profound changes will occur in our lives and we are not sure we are up to shouldering what feels like the burden of the unknown. Something inside of us fears the loss of normalcy and the familiar.

What gives us courage in the face of potential loss? What makes the changes worth it? Is the pattern we are weaving one that pictures liberation? If so, what risks are we willing to take with time, with color, with attention, with texture? Are we willing to risk a new sort of image for our lives?

Our own God Soul, our Holy Guardian Angel, our inner Genius, whispers to us, "Be not afraid." Can we breathe in some courage and breathe out some compassion, and take up the task at hand? Can we live fully, despite our fears? Can we use the energy of fear to propel us forward instead of using it as an excuse to keep us in place?

Can we move ever toward our sacred work?

What can we commit to today?

———

Author's note: for disabled or neurodivergent folks, I recommend skipping ahead to Chapter Seven and reading the short segment on "Honoring Your Body, Emotions, and Mind." It may help frame the rest of the course.

THIS COURSE

This is a simple eight-week course designed to help us establish a regular daily practice that works for our lives. It will encourage us to try different ways to connect with self and spirit each day. There are suggested readings from my book *Kissing the Limitless*, should you wish to expand upon the work in theory and practice, but those readings are not necessary.

Everything I do is affected by the presence or absence of daily practice. Success is more readily available, as is motivation, when I show up for myself each day. My students and clients, while they—as I did—sometimes struggle with establishing daily practice, also report that everything in their lives feels better, easier, and that they have more strength of will and presence to whatever arises, having made this first commitment: to the daily sitting with self and divinity in whatever form appears.

Daily practice supports their success.

Readers of this brief book are encouraged not to give up, to continue making attempts at these simple centering techniques and prods to presence and communion. If you miss a day, there is always the next.

I wish you steadfastness, curiosity, and enough self-love to return to the cushion, the altar, the page, or the mat. It is the most worthwhile activity I have ever done.

MORNINGS

You will notice that most often I write about practicing in the morning. The reason for this is that in doing so, we set the tone and template for our day. By taking time in the morning, before starting our work day—whatever that may look like—we begin from a place of center, stillness, and connection. This enables us to call upon these qualities throughout the day as we find need of them.

I recognize that some people really struggle to do *anything* in the morning. I'm not a great morning person myself, and have experimented with various forms of entering into daily practice. Currently, I rise, say a prayer, drink some water and take my medication, put the kettle on for tea, do some movement to get my blood, breath, and body moving, honor my ancestors and Gods, and then settle into a contemplation practice.

For years, the first thing I would do was meditation and self-observation. In other years, I would allow myself a shower first. In still other time periods, I would have a cup of tea and then meditate, but I stopped that practice because I found it became too easy to "check a few emails" while drinking my tea, and then all of a sudden I was lost in the flow of work.

In the time in which I'm updating this book —late 2017—a propensity for starting the day by checking social media, which also includes checking the news, causes a whole other host of problems. This can spiral a person into anxiety, anger, worry, longing, dismay, or simply scattered distraction.

Generally, if we begin sluggish, or anxious, or scattered, that is how our day will run, and it will require greater and greater efforts to bring us back to center, if we arrive at all.

Parents of young children will often say that mornings are no time for them to practice. For them, I recommend using whatever time they have in the bathroom to do some basic centering, breathing, and presence practices.

Other people arrive at work a little early and do meditation and devotional work via a slow walk in the park before entering their workplace, or by sitting in their car in the parking lot, attending to breath and prayer before heading into the office. Find what works for your life, but commit to doing *something* in the morning, even if it is only for a few minutes.

If you feel your morning practice isn't quite long enough or focused enough for your spiritual intentions, bracket your day with an evening practice.

Many people find candle gazing before bed to be calming and relaxing. Others do a daily inventory in the evenings, either through writing or thought, as a way to honor the day that has been. Still others light incense at their altars and give thanks for the day, and offer prayers for projects they are working on, or for the health and well being of their families.

I encourage a certain amount of flexibility in practice just to get us doing *something* foundational on a regular basis. That said, we must take care to not deviate too much, or too quickly, from our original plan, because this can be a sign that we are just resisting the practice altogether.

For years, for example, I said I could not meditate. In reality, I *would not* meditate because it felt like too difficult a task and deep down, in not meditating, I was able to avoid looking at some parts of myself that needed attention. Finally, a teacher in the Gurdjieff Work made sitting practice a requirement, and I sat my butt down. For this, I feel incredibly grateful.

Without sitting practice, my life and work would not have the richness and depth it does, nor would I have the ability to be present to such a wide variety of emotions, situations, or thoughts. I owe a great deal of my current joy and success to the simple—yet difficult—act of sitting still and breathing, observing what arose, and then letting it go.

In more recent years, the steadiness of my daily practice has helped me through big life shifts, deaths, moves, and career changes. Daily spiritual practice is the bedrock that supports my creative practices, my new publishing business, and my intimate relationships.

ON THE MEDITATIONS

I recommend reading the meditation sections through before going through the practices. You may even wish to record them and play them back in order to experience the meditation fully.

WEEK ONE

THOUGHTS ON CRAFT

"How is the craftsman, in the way in which he approaches his craft after twenty years as well as when he first begins, a student?" —Carla Needleman

What is craft? For me, the very word conjures up an image of a woman at the potter's wheel and a man at the lathe, a healer in his herb garden or a magician in her temple. Craft requires activity, study, and persistence.

For me, this study of craft requires daily practice: a continuing commitment to showing up—for myself and my Gods—in order to deepen, learn, and grow. This carries over into the practice of writing, of physical activity, and of relating to the world.

Some of our leaders and teachers do not maintain

daily practice. Consequently, we often see individuals whose power begins to twist inside of them in ways that are not helpful. They haven't developed a strong and supple base of personal power, so they try to hoard the power of the group, or grow jealous of the power they perceive in another person. This causes problems, and both they and their communities grow out of balance.

In order to grow stronger, we need a container for our energies. That container is best built by ongoing practice, self-observation, and learning how to connect outward from our center.

In our own lives, we can see how energy ebbs and flows, how our moods shift, how our effectiveness waxes and wanes, how we lose our center and return. What I have found in my own life is that my ability to center quickly is based on my commitment to my foundational practices.

These are practices that start my day, the basics that I am never without, that form the platform on which all else is built. They are different from the tools that are so well integrated that I have grown used to calling upon them at will. They also are different from things I used to know better than the back of my hand, but which have now fallen into disuse and sometimes even been forgotten.

Foundational practice is my core, and is something I'm ever returning to—a reminder, a rock, and something that requires me to practice.

Practice also requires me to take a risk every day. That risk is the ability to fully commit to myself, my life, my work and my Path, even if it is only for five or ten minutes in the morning. That five or ten minutes helps to make everything else possible.

As this course progresses, we will talk about our resistances to practice. This week, let us learn a couple of techniques. There are two exercises I would like us to practice: the still point work, and soul alignment.

SOUL ALIGNMENT

Though we are one being, we have many component parts.

Most spiritual traditions have ways to come back into states of alignment. I write about methods from my traditions both in *Kissing the Limitless* and *Evolutionary Witchcraft*.

Your tradition likely has some way of honoring or acknowledging your various parts and bringing them into conversation with one another. If we look at circle casting, for example, we can see that one facet of this action calls upon our mind, our energy, our emotions, our bodies, and our connection to spirit and asks all of these to be present for the rite at hand.

Kabbalists meditate on the Middle Pillar as the place the human and cosmos come into true. Heathens can find the World Tree reflected inside the self. Mystic Christians listen for the Still Small Voice within.

What are some examples from your own tradition?

For now, let us take in four breaths, fully inhaling, fully exhaling:

Take a deep breath to honor our physical bodies. Take in a breath to acknowledge the parts of self that are animal, instinct, and child. Breathe in and thank the parts that are human, rational, and relational. Breathe in and touch the parts that are connected to the ancestors, the Gods, and your own spark of divinity.

Now breathe deeply in, pause, fully exhale, pause. Do this two more times. Then tilt your head back and exhale the last breath upward as a prayer that all of your parts work together, united by intention to live a centered, effective life, woven together by the power of your breath.

MEDITATION

Somewhere between your navel and your pelvic bowl is a place of stillness. Take a breath, and invite your attention to drop into that space. Name that place your center. Take another breath into stillness, and imagine exhaling through every pore of your skin, out into the space around you—your auric body.

You have a center of stillness. You have space and flow around you. You can return to this by taking in one conscious breath and recalling for one moment that you are not anxiety, or rushing, or sadness, or that which is scattered.

You are now connected to the still point at your center. You can center around this stillness, any time you choose.

Take another breath.
Drop your attention.
Exhale out.
Straighten your spine if you can.
Do it all again.

SPIRITUAL PRACTICE, WEEK ONE

Julia Cameron pioneered the use of "Morning Pages" to get the flow moving in life. This can also be a helpful form of self-observation for some. The practice is that of automatic writing, also used by occultists who wanted to contact Spirit.

Do not let the pen stop moving across the page, or the fingers to cease typing, until you have written three pages. Do this first thing in the morning (after your tea or shower if need be, but before anything else).

Commit to writing three pages a day for six days this week.

If you are a person who has difficulty with writing practices, I recommend doing three simple drawings a day, or one collage. The point is not to make something that looks or feels perfect. The point is to work on something from a state of no-expectation of outcome. If you are drawing, don't let the pen or pencil leave the page. Keep your hand moving. If you are collaging, pick the first images that attract you, and start cutting and gluing. Don't pause to think about it.

Let the practice move through you, rather than attempting to control the practice.

Supplemental Reading:
Kissing the Limitless
"Learning to Center," pages 52-56, Chapter Three
"Sitting with Spirit," pages 66-67, Chapter Four

ALTARS

What rests upon the altar of your life? What are you making sacred with your presence?

We can infuse any activity with the scent of the sacred. How does our body touch the chair, how are hands and arms connected to our shoulders? We are present with our bodies as we type—trying to communicate across great distances. What happens when we pass a tree? Do we drink it in with our eyes? Do we say hello to the sparrows? We are present as we walk to work, or lunch, or home.

There is no place that is not holy ground. When we are present—oriented to East and West, North and South, oriented in and out—we find the sacred waiting, everywhere.

What practices connect you?

WEEK TWO

LONGING FOR CONNECTION

"When people go within and connect with themselves, they realize they are connected to the universe and they are connected to all living things." —Armand Dimele

What is it in you that longs for deeper connection? And what do you long for connection to: other humans, God Herself, Holy Nature, the Gods and Goddesses, creativity, the ancestors, your soul's work?

Take a few moments right now to close your eyes, breathe, and listen for this longing for connection. Try to sense the answers to both questions.

When we take time to listen to our longing, we give ourselves the opportunity to listen to a deep calling.

When we allow ourselves to open to a sense of connection, we also open to desire and to support for that desire. Practice strengthens that support.

We often struggle to show up to practice —and we will dive more deeply into our fears around that next week —but for now, I want to simply say this: practice is called practice because it is not meant to be perfect. It is there to set a foundation of help. It is our offering of time and attention to ourselves. Practice is, to put it simply, about practicing.

What would you like to practice in your life? Presence? Attention? Awareness? A feeling of centeredness? A return to a touchstone? Greater connection to your path? A clearer sense of self? Self-love and self-care?

Daily attention and effort can help with any of those. Can we think of our time commitments as a practice, rather than an end product or a chore? So much of our inner struggles comes around feeling imperfect, or impatience with something new. So we ask for the help of structure: a practice suggested by someone else that we try out for a time; a group to practice or check in with; a defined amount of time…. All of these are support beams rising from the foundation that is our initial commitment. Eventually, we build our monastery, our temple, or our home.

We are all seekers here. We are all following some distant star, and eventually we can come to recognize that this star resides in our very core.

This week, notice that in you that seeks. Notice that in you that signed up for this course of study. Notice that in you that longs to return to your self, your soul, your deeper life. Notice that in you that wants.

Let yourself open and sink a little deeper.

CULTIVATING CONSCIOUS PRESENCE

One of the benefits of regular practice is the cultivation of our ability to be present with our lives, in our communities and relationships, with our work, and with all the things we consider to be sacred.

Over time, for example, sitting with ourselves will show us how often we are *not* present in our lives. We will begin to notice the conversations going on in our heads, or the worry, or the fantasies that take us out of conditions that feel unbearable or are fraught with boredom or pain.

By increasing conscious presence, we increase our abilities to choose more clearly, and to notice what we want and what we desire.

All of this begins by observing and being with, rather than trying to avoid or change things that currently are.

. . .

I'd like to offer two techniques that have helped me. The first is drinking a cup of water in the morning. This is something I do every day, before prayers and sitting with myself.

When I began this practice, I used hot water with a squeeze of lemon in a cup that fit nicely in my hands. I would breathe quietly, noticing the sensation of the cup, the scent of lemon, and I would wait until the water became cool enough to drink. I drank it sip by sip, consciously. Slowly. This got me in touch with my body, with all of my senses, and with being in full presence with a simple task.

All of this, taken together, set my body, mind, and emotions up for the day to come in a gentle, supportive way.

These days, I pour myself a cup of water at night. In the morning, I stand in front of my altar, make some prayers, bless the water, and then take the thyroid medication that is currently increasing my health.

After this, if I want more time with water, I will mix boiling and room temperature water in a mug and drink it consciously and thankfully, before I have a cup of tea.

I use other practices of presence, too, which I also call "keys to remembrance." Before walking through a door, I take a centering breath.

I center and bless my food in silence, and then take a deep breath before having the first bite. If I'm in company, before the first drink at dinner, I raise my glass to toast the Gods and Goddesses. After either or both of these, I can enjoy conversation, or the book I may be reading, but I start every meal with conscious presence.

The more we cultivate the practice of presence, the more support we have to be present with every aspect of our lives.

And that is a good thing.

MEDITATION

Think about your day.

Think about your week.

Is there anything in your day or week that feels fuzzy, or barely formed?

Ask yourself the question: Was I present in that moment, or had I wandered far away?

Is there anything that makes you wince? Was I present in that moment, or had I wandered far away?

Take a deep breath. Soften your edges. Imagine you can send a breath through the space in your chest that cradles your heart. Take three, long, slow breaths, breathing in through your navel and out through your heart. In through your navel and out through your heart. In through your navel and out through your heart.

Now imagine what being present with each moment in your life feels like. Imagine a life where you can be in relationship with each conversation, each sip of water, each piece of music, and each friend.

Breathe in. Exhale.
Choose your life.

SPIRITUAL PRACTICE, WEEK TWO

Every morning this week, notice your still point. Align your soul with the cycles of four breaths. This should take one to three minutes.

Three days this week, write a letter or make a collage or drawing that is in dialogue with your Seeker, that part of you that longs for deeper connection. Ask it questions and listen for the answers.

One question to start us off could be, *"Seeker, what do you desire?"*

Write (or draw, or collage) for two to three pages, without letting the pen leave the page.

Schedule those days now: Monday, Wednesday, Friday, or Tuesday, Thursday, Saturday. Know in advance what three days you are committing to. This helps bolster intention.

A haphazard intention is no intention at all.

FURTHER ACTION

On the days you are not writing or drawing, practice consciously drinking a cup of warm water in the morning. Take the time to slow down at the beginning of the day by communing with water and your body.

Notice how the cup feels in your hands. Notice how the water feels in your mouth, and moving down your throat.

How amazing is it to be able to be present with a simple cup of water?

ALTARS

Place a cup of water on your altar. Refill it every week. Look at it every day. Let it remind you that you are mostly water. Your tears and spit, blood and sweat are sacred.

You can offer water to other beings, and to yourself.

You cannot accept more if you are filled to the top. You cannot pour if you are empty.

The cup reminds us of balance and flow.

Be with water.

WEEK THREE

THE POWER OF NOTICING

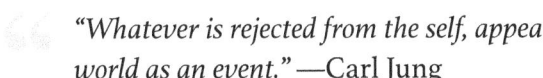 *"Whatever is rejected from the self, appears in the world as an event."* —Carl Jung

Spiritual practice opens us to noticing our lives and everything in them. Conversely, our lives help us to open to our spiritual practice.

If you are a person who is used to thinking of your life as an obstacle to spiritual practice, I invite you to drop your attention into the still point at your center and take a breath there.

Spiritual practice is not separate from our lives. It is part of it, whether we ignore it or not. Spirit has a way of bursting into life, interrupting thought and emotion, and sometimes bringing cataclysmic change.

Spirit bursts into our lives through music, dance, art, trees, ocean, and desert sky. Spirit bursts in on the laughter of friends or the tears of grief. Sometimes, spirit whispers to us in our most difficult moments.

Actively cultivating a relationship with spirit can be both revolutionary and life expanding. As said already, it can offer a sense of steadiness and well-being to our lives. It can also offer the ability to simply be more present with life in all of its varied splendor.

So, noticing our resistance—not trying to change it, just noticing it—expands our relationship with spiritual practice. It's another step in recalling who we are and where we are in our lives.

Do you habitually say, "I can't." Or, "That's too hard." Or, "I forgot." Or, "It makes me too uncomfortable." Or, "I just need to fix..."?

Does a feeling of tension, lethargy, anger, or illness fill your body when you think of committing to daily spiritual practice?

What emotions arise?

Do you only recall you were supposed to sit, or pray, or exercise hours after the scheduled time has passed?

We can notice.

Noticing is caring.

Noticing is a reminder.

Noticing shows us things about ourselves we never saw before.

Noticing is a spiritual practice.

NOTICING RESISTANCE

We're going to take our noticing practice one layer deeper. Ready or not...

Take a breath.

Think to yourself something along the lines of, *"I wish to commit to a daily spiritual practice. I wish to make a commitment to myself."* Whatever the exact words are, close your eyes for a moment, and listen to your interior being.

Where do you feel pockets of tension or resistance? In your emotions? In your mind? In your body?

Our body is a powerful teacher and often points to things we might be ignoring. Is there tension in your throat, shoulders, or abdomen? Does your breath seize up within you, or do you start to sweat?

Find the still place in your center and breathe into it. Let your exhalation open your attention to the tension or sense of resistance. Just be and breathe for a moment.

We start here, with the body. Then we can notice how we disconnect from our wish to show up, and examine the different forms resistance takes. Resistance comes in many forms: forgetfulness, anger, apathy, getting busy, cleaning the house, taking care of others, messing around on the Internet.... What are some of your methods? Along with in the body, where do you notice resistance in your thought processes and emotions?

Oftentimes we resist what we most deeply want. Or we resist what will be of the greatest help to our life's intentions.

This is different from assessing a plan or a situation and listening to the strong "No!" that might arise.

The resistance that I'm speaking of appears in all the ways we dance away from our desire, all the ways in which we undersell and undercut our time, dreams, and efforts.

We become like a child refusing to take the medicine that will cure her illness, or the two-year-old, exhausted, throwing a tantrum rather than allowing his parent to put him in bed so he can sleep. Another image I like is that of a puppy dragging on the leash rather than go for a walk.

What in us is like that fractious child or that puppy? What other parts of us *want* the self commitment that daily centering, prayer, yoga, or meditation might lend us?

Something tells me that we fear ourselves. What might confront if we cease avoiding the heartbeat of our practice?

Something also tells me that we fear the depths of our power, grace, and beauty. Who will be responsible for the results of our risks if we show up with full presence?

If we do not commit to ourselves, who will?

MEDITATION

Close your eyes. Slow your breathing down. Imagine the edges of your body growing lighter. Let your attention drop into stillness at your center, and for now, allow any worries you might have to float away.

What is the life that you desire? If you could seek that with all your heart, what might your life look like? Feel like? Taste like? Sounds like?

Who would you be?

Notice your response to these questions. Take in another deep breath. Exhale.

What do you allow yourself to wish for? What wants to run away?

Hold out your hands. Imagine that your left hand can grasp the hand of the part of you that wishes. Imagine that your right hand can reach out and hold the hand of the parts of you that want to run away. Notice how these hands feel in yours.

Talk to the part of you that has wishes and desires. Tell it what you hope for. Tell it what you fear. Now turn to the part of you that wants to run away. Ask it what it hopes and what it fears. Feel all of these questions and answers inside of you.

Now open your eyes.

Take all of this information to your altar. And ask yourself, "What is my practice?"

What would your life be like if, every time you had a longing or desire, you took that to your altar? What would happen if you allowed practice to support your desire? What might you seek then? And what might you resist?

Honor this. Honor all of this.

Our practices can embrace anything; we just need to remember to show up.

SPIRITUAL PRACTICE, WEEK THREE

Continue with the daily still point and soul alignment work.

Then try out this technique, which is a form of devotional practice that appears in many traditions such as Judaism, Sufism, Hinduism, Paganism, and Christianity, to name five.

Pick a name of power, a God form you work with, or something else that works for you as a verbal focus. You may wish to sit very still for this, or you may wish to stand and rock your body, or do the practice while walking. You may wish to have eyes closed or open. Play around with it and notice what your spirit wants.

The name could be "Freyja, Freyja, Freyja," or "Blessed Nature, Blessed Nature, Blessed Nature" or "Yod Heh Vov Heh" or anything else you choose as your focus for the week. Let this chanting be any ally in working with your resistance.

Let it be a reminder of your connection to the sacred.

Allow your body to move as it will, and let your voice rise.

Supplemental Reading:
Kissing the Limitless
"Cultivating Practice," pages 19-23, Chapter One
"Feeding Our Will," pages 123-127, Chapter Six
"Feeling, Not Being," pages 153-155, Chapter Eight

FURTHER ACTION

Though our main practice this week is simply *noticing* our resistance, I also invite you to write a dialogue or make some art around working with your Resistor, just as you did with your Seeker.

Again, pick three days to do this writing. Schedule them right now. Notice if even scheduling makes something squirm.

It's all just information.

ALTARS

A student once wrote: *I am ready now to commit to sitting at the altar daily, but it still bothers me that in times of stress and challenge, I scale my practice back, just when I need to be doing more.*

I responded: *Good for you for re-committing.*

Scaling back when we need more is pretty common. It is good to notice the tendency and then ask ourselves, "What is one thing we can do to feed our practice so it can support us?" That way, rather than giving up completely, we may say "I will sit at my altar, light a candle, breathe and center. After three minutes, I can go about my day." This eases up on the struggle to "do it all or do nothing" that so many end up in.

WEEK FOUR

SELF-OBSERVATION

The main thing I have learned in years of practice—and practicing at practice!—is to just notice, as we started doing last week.

The process of observation helps me realize that everything is simply information—not good, not bad.

Training my mind to take things as information then helps deepen the ongoing process of noticing.

When I want to label things, or make value judgments, I'm naturally going to encounter parts of myself that I simply do not want to notice, so why should I try?

Removing value judgments—or arresting the process by noticing our tendency to judge—brings us to a place in our practice where things just *are*. This frees us up to say, "Isn't that interesting, the way I go back to this thought loop or that physical process of avoidance?"

Our curiosity can be piqued and we can become scientists or explorers of being. In contrast, saying things such as, "I'm a bad person for feeling/thinking/acting in such and such a way," stunts our curiosity, and therefore limits our wish to return to presence.

Who wants to be present for such a weak-willed, stupid, mean, or lazy person? As we can see, some of the process around noticing and arresting judgment will require observing things we traditionally don't like about ourselves.

I would be remiss in not mentioning that for still others of us, we don't want to admit to or notice ways in which we shine.

What parts of your personality want to label things? Training ourselves to notice what is beneath our judgments is a process I sometimes call "listening on a level deeper."

When I observe a knee-jerk reaction, I like to take a breath and observe what parts want to call this thing *good* or *acceptable* and that other thing *bad* or *not acceptable*.

What is the agenda? Does one part then get to feel superior, or safer, or get to tell a beloved story about how we are and who we are?

Let's try to notice when we are weaving a story.

Right now, take a breath.

Just notice.

FURTHER WORK WITH OBSERVATION

Just as we noticed our seeking and our resistance, we can notice other patterns.

What are your patterns of speech, energy, emotion, and body?

Starting with energy:

What sort of energy does your life feed right now?

Does it feed speeding up, worry, sloth and enervation, defeat, triumph, love, excitement, engagement, apathy, frustration, self-righteousness, anger...?

What sort of energy would you like to cultivate? When you imagine yourself in your best life, what does that feel like or look like?

This is also just information.

Do your life and habits eat your energy?

Do your life and habits increase vital energy?

Do your life and habits drain your energy?

Do your life and habits increase frenetic, fractious energy?

. . .

Expand this out, over time, to include the other facets of self-observation:

Notice your patterns of thought and speech.

Notice your patterns of sleep, eating, drinking, exercising, posture.

Notice your emotional patterns.

Don't try to change anything. Just notice.
Then ask: Do these patterns serve my life?

MEDITATION

Take a deep breath. Find your center.

Think about your day. Let your breath come slow and easy, and try to imagine yourself in every situation you found yourself in this day. Or yesterday.

As you imagine yourself going about your daily activities, notice how your body feels. Notice if tension has crept in, or if your breathing has changed. Notice your posture and feel the expression on your face.

Notice any emotional spikes or dips. Notice any energetic changes. Try to remember what you thought about, or what you said.

Take another deep breath. Drop your attention even more deeply inside of you. And ask yourself the question, "What are my patterns?" With your breath as your guide, slowly examine first your patterns of speech. Then notice your emotional state. Did your emotions on this day feel or seem typical? Or did something occur to shift them? What thoughts do you notice that are attached to those emotional states? How does this affect your body?

How is the examination of this affecting your body, your energy, your emotions, and your breath right now?

Are these states of being how you usually live?

Are these states of being how you wish to live?

Inhale as deeply as you can, then pause. Exhale as fully as you can, then pause. Allow these pauses to become openings, a chance for something new to appear. Breathe in this way at least three more times, or for as long as it feels right.

Say these words if they feel helpful: "I wish to know myself. I wish to feel the fullness of my life. May I honor whomever I am, in this moment in time. Blessed be."

SPIRITUAL PRACTICE, WEEK FOUR

Use of candles as a spiritual focus is very common in many spiritual traditions. Candles engage the non-verbal parts of ourselves, alerting them to the fact that something special is about to happen.

To light a candle is to set aside space and time, delimiting the ordinary and imbuing it with a sense of the sacred. Whether the ritual of lighting birthday candles, or lighting candles to denote that tonight's meal is special, or lighting candles to signal the beginning of a religious service, we understand that candle lighting is in itself a significant act.

For this practice, pick any sort of candle you like, just make sure it is large enough to burn for five to ten minutes at a time. If you have a favorite color, choose that.

Never leave a candle burning unattended, not even a jar candle.

Stand or sit in front of your candle. Find the still point in your center.

Then light the candle. If you like, you may set the intention that the candle will help deepen your connection to spiritual practice, and toward creating a spiritual home for yourself.

But you can also simply strike a match, touch it to wick, and watch the flame.

Slow your breathing down. Allow your eyes to rest upon the flame. Breathe. Gaze at the candle for five minutes. Then take another deep breath, and allow your gaze to soften further. You may even close your eyes if you wish. Sit and breathe for another five minutes, with the candle flame as your companion.

Refocus your eyes on the flame.

Extinguish the wick.

Take in another deep inhalation and then exhale.

Align your soul.

Do this practice for six out of the seven days this week.

Supplemental Reading:
   Kissing the Limitless
   "Gauging the Real," pages 29-36, Chapter Two

FURTHER ACTION

This week, start off by simply noticing what happens when you engage (or try to engage) with practice.

What trips you up and what draws you in?

Look back on the last two weeks and see what you can notice in retrospect. Now look at how your current week goes for a few days.

Note down in two columns, one for "good" and one for "bad," all the things you notice. Look at those lists, and either cut off the top headers or decorate them into obscurity (draw flowers and planets over them until you can't read the words anymore).

At the bottom, write across both columns: "This is all information."

ALTARS

"There are two ways of spreading light: to be the candle or the mirror that reflects it." – Edith Wharton

Dedicate a candle on your altar specifically for candle gazing. Pick a color that reminds you of your dedication to your path.

Light that candle every day. Gaze into the flame. Breathe.

WEEK FIVE

SHIFTING PATTERNS

> *"I learned that not making a decision is in itself a decision—and that my fear of change was actually a fear of failure."* —Maria Cristina McDonald

Sometimes what seem to be separate patterns have, over the years, banded together to form complexes: nexuses of emotional, mental, psychological, and physical tendencies that end up being quite strong. They can control the rest of our lives.

The past two weeks, we spent time noticing. This week, we will continue this by attempting to observe how some of our patterns flow into each other, and support or undermine each other.

Is there a part of us that wants to eat a whole pint of ice cream or bag of chips, or watch too much TV, or to go to the gym for two hours every day, or work constantly...? Does this pattern that we notice show us a resistance to doing daily practice, or healthy exercise, or resting, or drawing/painting/dancing, or speaking honestly with our dear friends?

Does a wish to create, or connect, or feel healthy show us a desire to engage in practices that support our lives?

What are *your* patterns? What do *you* notice? They will be different for each of us.

What systems have your various parts been building together? Can you begin to unravel these threads and loosen some of the knots?

Slow your breathing down. Think on your life, as it is right now. What do you notice? What feelings or images arise?

What patterns emerge?

Follow those patterns. Trace their power. Breathe.

Then let them go...

In looking at patterns and complexes, we tend to focus on what feels hard or "negative," so this week, I'd also like us to look at the patterns that feel like they support the wish for connection and the patterns that are working to uphold our commitment.

Let us revisit the wish that brought us to this course in the first place. What patterns or processes can we honor this week that will help to strengthen our wish? How can we recommit? We are at the point where recommitment is necessary. Remember your wish. Bow to your wish.

Patterns that undermine self-love can often distance us from our deep wishes, desires, and commitments. Can you do something this week that shows your love for self, as a being worthy of love in and of yourself, and as a being worthy of love?

Keep breathing, whether this feels satisfying or difficult. Keep noticing. Find a way to strengthen and support your wish.

ON CLEANSING

 "The cure for anything is salt water: sweat, tears or the sea." —Isak Dinesen

Most traditions have cleansing practices. They are important, and can help us come back to ourselves when life feels muddy or difficult, or we just want extra clarity.

Some people like sacred baths. I love them to, and use them often. It's a great thing to offer ourselves that time to sit, soak, breathe, and pray. But other times, the elaborateness of a sacred bath gets in the way. We don't have the resources, or we won't make the time.

A shower with a salt scrub is another great cleansing practice. So is conscious hand-washing. Pause. Breathe. Be with the water and our bodies. To be truly present as we do such a simple task is very powerful.

Any basic cleansing practice from your tradition will

do. We can cleanse with breath, with wind, with water, with salt, with incense, and with sound. The purpose of cleansing is to release that which has been bound up, freeing up that life force for other uses.

Begin by noticing, and then open to the life energy that is tied up in your patterns and complexes.

MEDITATION

Imagine a warm summer's day. Imagine you are perfectly safe.

Take your worries, your anger, your sorrow, your anxiety or fear, your sense of defeat, and carry it with you. Carry them with you.

Imagine you are at the head of a long dock leading to a lake. Imagine the sound of the water, lapping at the dock posts. Imagine the calm, blue-gray water just ahead. Imagine the trees that surround the lake. Hear the sounds of birds, and the splash of fish.

Imagine that you can take everything you carry, and move down the dock from the shore to the water, and ease yourself into the lake. Remember, you are safe here. Nothing can harm you right now.

Imagine you are floating on this lake. The water is cool and refreshing, but not cold. The sun is warm on your face. Your body is completely relaxed; your breath flows easily, smoothly, and surely. It lifts your belly, and fills your lungs. It is almost as though your breath can reach all the way from the soles of your feet, to the tips of your fingers, to the crown of your head.

Your only job right now is to float.

Your only job right now is to let go.

Allow any anxiety, fear, sorrow, anger, worry, or sense of defeat to release their hold on you and float away into the waters of the lake.

Let yourself feel cradled and held. Allow the waters of this lake to buoy you up, to surround you, to support you. Just. Let. Go.

Float. Breathe. Be.

SPIRITUAL PRACTICE, WEEK FIVE

We can re-ingest the power bound up in the patterns we have observed by breathing them back in, or by literally breathing them into a cup of water and drinking them back, in an unbound form.

How to do this via breath: Hold in your mind the patterns that tie you up and impede your daily practice (or any other practices). Breathe into the stillness in your center. As you exhale, imagine these patterns slowly unknotting themselves. As they unknot, the power and energy held within them will release itself into your being, starting with the physical body, and emanating out into the energy fields around your physical form.

Each time you breathe in, more and more of this unbound power is taken back in along with the life energy ever present all around us. The more of this power we can inhale, the more energy is available to loosen the knots inside.

I call this sort of practice "the rite of unbinding" and often use a cup of water as an aid. Breathe in life. Breathe what is bound up inside into a cup of water. Do this continuously until it feels done for the moment. Then pause and say a prayer, asking for clarity and healing. Then breathe a blessing over the cup of water.

Drink it in.

FURTHER ACTION

Continue with still point work and soul alignment.

Notice how your patterns feed each other.

Do a daily cleansing practice: rite of unbinding, breathing and unknotting, salt scrub, or some other spiritual cleansing.

Notice supportive patterns.

Contract to practice six days.

Find something that inspires you!

Supplemental Reading:
Kissing the Limitless
"Looking for Longevity" and "Replacing the Rote with Intention," pages 42-46, Chapter Three
"Tracing Complexity," pages 109-110, Chapter Five
"Loving the Self," pages 204-205, Chapter Ten

ALTARS

"Sometimes we need to stop doing in order to open to our Being.
   We cannot create the life that we desire if there is no room for silence." – from *Make Magic of Your Life*

When do you listen to your Gods?
   When do you listen to your heart and soul?
   When do you pause to ask what is underneath this emotion, or that sense of hurry?
   How well do you allow yourself to root into your life?
   Without the power of silence, we cannot choose, we can only react, because we've made no space to sense or know what we want, or what feels right.
   Without cultivating the power of silence in our lives, we lose out on presence. When we are not present with what is, we become trapped in cycles of worry or regret. We are always assigning labels to things to help us keep track of what we may or may not want. It becomes harder

and harder to see past the labels to how things actually are. It becomes easier to let the world choose for us, rather than for us to choose the world.

WEEK SIX

PHYSICAL INTEGRATION

"Wisdom, creativity, and love are discovered as we relax and awaken through our bodies."
—Tara Brach

For me, practice should always aim toward the integration of all of our parts and the expansion of our capacity to be kinder, more creative, more aware, and more powerful human beings.

Our bodies are directly linked to mental, emotional, and spiritual well-being. We have great potential, much of it often languishing because of habit, emotional complexes, or background. Our bodies can help us step more fully into integration if we pay attention to them. We began with our observations of physical tension occurring in response to resistance. Now, I'd like to discuss how we can allow the body to be an ally to our work in other ways.

Because the overculture sends us convoluted messages about our bodies, exercise, food, how to look, dress, and (not) age, many of us resist actively courting physical health, or we struggle with it off and on, trapped in systems of self-loathing, or thinking we "should" do this or that.

I encourage us all to take a deep breath and ascertain whether or not we can apply the thoughts of practice and self-commitment to our physical forms as well. The more we can do this, the greater our chance of coming into alignment and getting all of our parts on board the train of practice, presence, and spiritually powerful lives.

Physical engagement and awareness is spiritual activity. Not only does this include yet another part of self in our quest for wholeness and a happy life, exercise or other forms of supportive physical engagement can also actively support our practices of meditation, centering, and presence.

There are many studies that show how regular exercise helps combat insomnia, mild depression, and some attention deficit or compulsive behaviors. Serotonin, dopamine. and endorphins are all affected by exercise. Used in concert with whatever medications or foods you may need, these can all help to regulate our brain chemistry.

This may not work for everybody. As with anything, experiment.

How has this worked in my own life? The more basic exercise I get, the easier it is to meditate and to keep showing up to practice because my brain is calmer and my emotions are less volatile. That said, I went through years where I pushed my body too hard and had to learn to ask myself what activity was truly most supportive.

We do not have to be a certain weight or size. We do not have to be ambulatory. All we need to do is to engage our bodies to the very best of our abilities.

You know your own body, so you know whether what is best for it is walking, stretching, getting a massage, lifting weights, dancing, drinking more water, taking a nap....

How can you support a healthy relationship with your body?

Whatever you choose, bring it into the realm of daily spiritual practice.

Body and spirit are not separate from one another. The more we remember this, the better able we are to bring our lives into a place of wholeness.

HONORING YOUR BODY, EMOTIONS, AND MIND

I can write only from my own experiences, and draw upon the experiences of some of my clients and students.

Everybody has different physical abilities.

Everyone has varied mental and emotional strengths, weaknesses, and differences.

I also know that, no matter how many times I say "adjust these practices to suit you," expectations and judgments may arise. Shame or frustration or the wish to give up may arise.

All of that is okay. All of that highlights the fact that we live in a culture that values production and work over deep well-being. And I easily fall prey to that as well.

I spent years fighting chronic pain. I've also spent years fighting a compromised immune system. I've seen people's judgments at my "getting sick a lot" and felt impatient with myself for the same despite doing my utmost to stay healthy.

Daily practice supported me then and is *still* part of what supports me.

Daily spiritual practice has increased my overall sense of well-being. It also helps me deal with internal judgments that arise when I feel I'm not doing enough, or when being sick feels like a failure.

So here's the key: sometimes we avoid certain daily practices because a part of our personality wants to hide. It fears exposure or change. And so we resist. Other times we avoid certain daily practices because they truly are not the correct practices for our bodies or minds.

How do we ascertain the difference? We listen. We observe. We practice. We start with one minute of breathing if that's all we can manage. We work up to five minutes of breathing and centering. We do that for three weeks and sense what happens.

We start with gentle stretching six days a week, and sense what happens.

We begin with one drawing a day and sense what happens. Or we set aside time for one collage a week, and sense what happens. Then we make time to sit quietly with that collage every day for five minutes…and we sense what happens.

Let practice be your laboratory. By approaching practice with as much curiosity as possible, we create an opening for discovery.

This course offers a variety of practice so we can try on different things. I recommend you try some if not most of these practices. I also recommend you look at your life and notice what other practices you may already have that you can commit to doing consciously and regularly.

For some people, it may be choosing to take the stairs instead of the elevator. For other people, it may be choosing to take the elevator instead of the stairs. The important thing is pausing, and then choosing. That's a practice.

For some people, it may be working up to sitting with ourselves for twenty minutes at a time, because we need to face ourselves in all our parts, and not run away.

For others it may be allowing ourselves to lie flat on our backs and imagine floating on a lake for ten minutes. When I went through a phase of terrible burnout, that is exactly what I did. My sitting practice turned into "floating on the lake" practice.

When my undiagnosed autoimmune disorder got truly debilitating, all I could do some days were say a prayer and center throughout the day. But I was still committed to practice.

That's what counts.

Once I was finally diagnosed, I charged my medicine up at the full moon, and placed the bottle on my altar where it remains. My first practice every day now is drinking water and taking a pill and then some herbs. My other practices follow from there.

Honor yourself. Let practice be a homecoming. Find the practices that honor *your* connection to spirit. Not mine.

I have recommended practices for certain types of spiritual work. Sitting, centering, and self observation are the core of those practices.

I have to admit that there may be other practices that neurodivergent people, or people with mental, emotional, or physical disabilities need. I came to understand my own neurodivergence very late, and what works for me may not work for everyone else.

What matters is showing up for ourselves as best we can.

Days when, as one person puts it "you are fighting your mind tooth and nail," perhaps allow yourself the practice of lighting a candle and taking three breaths, then extinguishing the candle. That's it.

Or allow yourself to gently rock or sway as you sit with yourself or say your prayers.

Or allow yourself the practice of pulling one Tarot card or rune. Or look at your favorite sacred image and take three breaths. Or find a piece of music or a place in nature that makes you feel connected and be with that for five minutes while trying to return to your center.

Set yourself up for support.

That's it.

Magic begins where we are.

Practice begins where we are.

Connection begins where we are.

And I wouldn't have it any other way.

MEDITATION

Inhale deeply. Exhale slowly. Isn't it amazing that you can breathe at all? Honor your breath. Inhale and say "thank you." Exhale and say "thank you." Inhale and say "thank you." Exhale and say "thank you."

If you can, place two fingers over the pulse in your neck. Allow your breath to rise and fall. Find the pattern of your pulse. One. Two. Three. Four. Count that pattern. Drop your attention deeper. Notice how the rhythm of your breath weaves in and out, dancing with the rhythm of your heart.

Isn't this marvelous? Every system in the body works in its own way. Every system of the body learns to work with other systems, in concert.

Peptides reach for one another. Cells divide. Blood flows. Synapses fire. Even when things go awry, our bodies still make music.

Begin to move to this rhythm. Perhaps your arms will sway, or your feet will tap. Perhaps your body will rock, or your fingers will make swirling motions in the air. It doesn't matter whether you are sitting, standing, or lying down, immerse yourself in the rhythm of the physical. Small motions or large, let your body move.

Say, or sing, or whisper these words to yourself: "Blessed be my body, child of this earth. Blessed be my body, child of this earth."

SPIRITUAL PRACTICE, WEEK SIX

This week, we will try another experiment: before sitting in meditation/self-observation practice for ten minutes, we will commit to ten to fifteen minutes of stretching, dancing, yoga, deep breathing, or walking. Remember: adjust the practice to whatever it is your particular body can do.

We will also continue to do the still point meditation and soul alignment every day. This is an entry point. The common recommendation for daily physical exercise is half an hour. If you wish to work up to this, I encourage it, but for this week, let us start with ten to fifteen minutes.

For those with physical limitations, do what you can, as you can. If what you can manage is sending breath and energy throughout your body, do that.

Supplemental Reading:

Kissing the Limitless
"Committing to Health" and "Celebrating the Body," pages 73-76, Chapter Four

FURTHER ACTION

Schedule two writing or drawing sessions. In the first session, write a letter to your body, emotions, or your mind. In the second session, let your body, emotions, or mind write a letter to you. Engaging in dialogue is helpful practice. We all need it.

WEEK SEVEN

SEEKING AND RESISTING

"Daily sitting is our bread and butter, the basic stuff of dharma. Without it we tend to be confused." —Charlotte Joko Beck

How do your wish and resistance feel now?

At this point in our exploration, we should have become better acquainted with both our wish and our resistance.

Remember your Seeker. It longs for depth and connection. It is a guide for your spiritual life. Remember those parts of you that are frightened or in states of avoidance. They still need to be listened to and brought to the project of your centering, your purpose, your gentleness, and your strength.

Take a breath and find your Seeker. Take another breath and find that in you that resists.

Write (or draw, or collage) at least two mornings on

each of these, for two pages each. What does your seeker have to tell you now? What words flow from your resistance? How do your emotions respond to both of these? Can you find your still point and align your soul?

As for practice, what methods (sitting, candle gazing, morning pages, chanting) are you finding yourself drawn to and what methods do you dislike? Why? Notice whether this is because they feel easy or hard, or because they are bringing you up against (or helping you avoid) various patterns of resistance.

Really try to gauge your responses and motivations. What practices do you think might be most fruitful for your spiritual growth over time? Remember that practice is about committing to yourself and supporting your life, bringing you further into balance and giving you greater resources to draw upon over time.

As a personal note, though I resisted sitting practice for many years, and then spent almost as many years struggling with the practice, I have found it to be one of the most illuminating and helpful foundational practices of all.

Sitting with myself became my spiritual companion, my champion, and my best mirror. The cushion or bench made it impossible to avoid myself, and therefore, I was able to bring more of my parts to light and integration. I feel grateful for this practice, despite its great difficulty. Persevering in the face of difficulty enabled me to sense the depth of my commitment to practice and to self. This has proven to be valuable as new challenges and learning curves arise.

For example, my experience with sitting practice has been a huge support in my practice of writing novels. I can center, pay attention to the manuscript, and produce a lot of words, whether I "feel like it" on any given day or not.

What do you think will help you the most? Is it prayer? Breath work? Conscious eating? Sitting practice? Soul alignment?

Reconnect with your breath and still point throughout the day, particularly as you work with any of the above questions. Try to be honest with all your parts of self and soul.

CORE AND BOUNDARY

Committing to daily practice is a way to continuously return to our centers and a way to establish and maintain our boundaries.

I often call this "center and circumference" work.

We don't need to "fix" things. Fixing is an outside-in process. Outside of ourselves. Outside of our communities. Outside of our families.

Centering brings us into the strongest and most supple places we have. It provides an anchor. That is true in the self. That is true in family. That is true in community.

What is the center of your community? How do community members connect to that? Can you bring that to consciousness?

The same practice is reflected within.

Communities, families, and the self also need boundaries. Sometimes those come in the form of agreements. Other times those come in the form of space and time.

If our boundaries are not connected to an anchor or a

center, they become brittle and can shatter or become traps.

The meditation that follows is another practice to use throughout the day.

When you need it, you can check in on one breath cycle. One inhalation. One exhalation.

You'll have help from your own soul. You'll have offered yourself the gift of time and breath.

You will be able to face what is in front of you from a more complete state.

And you can do this at any time, just by imagining your breath centering you and tracing the edges of your own personal boundary.

If we can claim our own space, we can more easily share space.

By knowing where we are, we can orient to community and to the cosmos.

MEDITATION

Imagine your personal center, that still point at your core. Now imagine your boundary. Imagine first, the boundary closest to your skin. Imagine it as a sheath of energy that traces the outline of your physical form.

Now imagine another boundary, further out. Do you have one? If not, imagine one. If yes, what shape is it in? Check in. Imagine you can sense how far out from your physical body it rests. Imagine if it seems in good repair.

Now imagine that, on a breath, you can subtly begin to shift your relationship with that boundary.

Breathe into your center.

Do that three more times.

As you exhale, imagine you lend life force to the edge of your boundary. Imagine you can smooth the edges.

Imagine your circumference as whole and light, yet strong. Imagine it egg-shaped or spherical.

Once done, practice dropping into still center on an inhalation, and shoring up, activating, and smoothing your circumference on an exhalation.

Do that three times.

SPIRITUAL PRACTICE, WEEK SEVEN

Every day, practice tuning into your still point and align your soul. Connect with your center and circumference, core and boundary.

Do five minutes of chanting or candle gazing, or stretching, or morning pages.

Sit with yourself and your breath for fifteen minutes. Don't worry about "quieting the mind." Just keep breathing, and keep re-centering, gently. Observe who you are, where you are.

Physically, it helps if your knees are below your pelvis and your spine can float up from there, but make whatever adjustments your body needs.

FURTHER ACTION

How will you recommit to daily practice? How will you support your wish? Here are some ideas:

First, write a contract with yourself to practice all six days this week.

Second, find something that inspires the parts of you that want to connect. Listen to a favorite piece of music, or write out a quote that you find particularly appealing. Take a long walk in a favorite place outside. Look at art.

Do whatever feels good to your soul's work.

WEEK EIGHT

TIME AND PRACTICE

"Everything is practice." —Pele

Practice makes possible.

Practice takes time, and we can make time for practice.

The reality is that practice also increases our ability to live in time and to feel time's spaciousness. When we pay attention to ourselves and the sacred every day, the sacred infuses our lives. That sense offers greater ease, strength, and flexibility to every facet of our lives.

So, even through struggle, practice becomes a great gift.

This course is coming to a close, but hopefully—with will and intention—our individual work shall continue. We shall remind ourselves that we want to show up for our lives in fullness and care. Keep opening to self-love in this work. Even if it feels difficult, know that it is part of what keeps the Seeker going. You can want something better for yourself: something finer, more engaged, more direct.

In changing relationship with yourself, you change your relationship with the world.

This week, as part of courting your Seeker and honoring your resistance, do one nice thing for yourself: buy flowers or a good piece of chocolate, take a bath, go for a walk in the woods, be fully present while making love...whatever it is, do it.

KEEPING PRACTICE FRESH

Practice does require repetition. It is tempting to decide something simply doesn't work for us, when really, we haven't allowed the practice to work *on* us yet. Our personalities have decided they don't like it, or they're bored, or it's stupid, or they don't wanna.

So we return to the practice, again and again. For three months. For six months. For one year. Sometimes for ten.

And yes, at a certain point, that practice can become rote. At a certain point, we may need to alter the practice or set it aside for a time.

I'll go back to my example from the beginning of the book: sitting practice. For years, I said I couldn't sit, I wouldn't sit, it did nothing for me...on and on, I avoided the simple yet dangerous practice of sitting myself down and breathing.

Then I studied under a teacher who required it. Twenty minutes daily, I had to sit in self observation. This was not about "quieting the mind" or "taming the emotions." This was about me, sitting on a cushion, and breathing with my thoughts, my emotions, my foot falling asleep and my back aching.

I hated it.

It has done more for me than any other practice. It trained me to look at myself and face the truth.

And yes, sitting for enough years eventually led to a calmer, more spacious mind, to greater emotional equanimity, and to the cultivation of a sense of inner stillness. But mostly? It helped me know myself.

After a spiritual breakthrough—brought on by practice, stress, and a combination of many things—sitting also brought immediate bliss. Whereas I used to sit for twenty minutes to two hours, I cut back to ten minutes. Then to five.

What I needed was the practice of centering. Sitting no longer led to the observation of different parts of self, it led to what some traditions call samadhi. That was great, and nourishing, but not what I felt I needed.

So sitting became a touchstone for me. I still sat daily, but no longer with the attention and rigor that I brought to it before.

That was one shift.

There have been other practices that I've done deeply for six months to a year at a time, and then cycled back out of again. Then, three years later, they would cycle back.

The important thing about changing up our practices is to remember *why* we practice. It isn't for entertainment or for punishment.

As a matter of fact, it's going to be for different reasons for us all.

My main objective, and what I've tried to teach others, is to use practice to become more self-aware and centered in our lives. Everything is built from our practices then. All the arcs of our lives, large or small, are predicated on the way we approach practice.

Practice, as I so often say, is foundational.

For others of us, though, practice will become the foundation of our relationship with the Gods, or with our particular creative forms, or our service to our communities.

So, if practice is feeling stale or rote, first ask, "Is there a way I can re-connect to this practice right now?"

And then ask, "What purpose does this practice serve?"

If you then choose a new practice, contract with yourself to do it for a minimum three-month cycle. Then check in again.

See how things feel.

Meditation

Slow your breathing down. Notice the edges of your energy field. Relax your body as much as you can.

Breathe deeply. Drop your attention into the place of stillness at your center.

Imagine that at your core is a stone well, surrounded by green grass. Peer into the well. Notice your reflection in the dark water. This is a well at which you can ask any question, and receive any answer. It is a well connected to your deepest wisdom. It is the place your ancestors and

Gods whisper, and your soul replies. It is the nexus of past, present, and future.

Be with this well. Drink of its waters. Feel the connection your weeks of practice provide.

The world around this well is rich, but often hurried. Here is a place where you can slow down. Be quiet. Center.

It is a place beyond place, in a time beyond time.

Feel your practices. Your ability to center and be present, increasing. The candles you have lit. The sacred names you have called upon.

In one of your hands rests a stone. It can carry any thought or question to the bottom of the well, to the deepest of the deep.

Think of what you might like to tell your wisdom, or what question you may want to ask of it.

Breathe that thought or question across the surface of the stone. Three times, breathe it across the surface.

Then drop the stone. Let go of the thought or the question.

Be and breathe.

Listen.

Let your wisdom answer.

SPIRITUAL PRACTICE, WEEK EIGHT

Commit to doing soul alignment and still point every day and do some other practice for twenty minutes, five to six days a week: sitting, chanting, candle gazing, morning pages, yoga....

Talk to the parts of your soul—your Seeker and Resistor, your animal soul, your intellect, and divine connection—and get them to sign on to a practice contract. What will it take to bring everyone on board? To lend all of their energy to this commitment?

Write a three-month contract to yourself.

Magical contracts are often written in red, hearkening to the time when a sacred compact was sealed with a drop of blood. I find it helpful to write out practice contracts in regular ink (whether by hand or electronically) and then print the final draft in red ink.

Pick a practice to stick with for the three months, to enable you to really sink into it, and start to sense where it might take you and what it might teach you. This can be one practice (e.g., sitting for twenty minutes) or a combination (e.g., morning pages and candle gazing, or yoga and sitting).

The only one who can commit to your life and your growth is you. What are you waiting for?

Supplemental Reading:
Kissing the Limitless
"Struggling to Connect," pages 118-119, Chapter Six

ALTARS

This week, the persimmons are ripe and the birds are everywhere.

I watch from my office window, occasionally venturing out, trying to get closer to the tree without disturbing the birds alighting there. Crows, large and black against the bare branches and bright orange globes, digging into the fruit, ripping open the flesh, eating. Then robins. Jays. Brown towhee. They peck at the openings the crows have made. Next come the sparrows. Starlings. Finches. Phoebe. The surprising arrival of cedar waxwings, dandies among the rest.

I listen. I watch. I breathe. I learn to be.

Inner listening is important, but so is tuning to what is around us. Both are vital to the examined life, because the examined life moves in the context of land, sky, factories, noise, concrete, and the great silence of the stars. What reminds you to listen? What drops you toward silence? To what or to whom do you pray?

When you make an altar of your life, everything becomes sacred.

COMING FULL CIRCLE

INTEGRATING PRACTICES

Many of the practices in this book can be threaded throughout your day: conscious presence —which includes breath, food, drinking water, and any other activity you choose—soul alignment, and center and circumference.

There are still other practices that you may wish to add in daily, or that may become monthly or weekly practices instead.

All of our daily practices, for example, help us to better attune ourselves to the cycles of moon and sun, and to pay attention to the seasons, to animals, to other human beings. Sometimes we wish to honor those connections directly, in ritual or prayer. Other times it is enough to pause and notice, "There is a full moon in the sky tonight." Or "The tree frogs have returned."

Just as practices may cycle, practices also tune us to the cycles all around us.

I have an ancestor altar that I spend time with every day. It used to be that I only had a couple of photographs that would sit on an altar all year. Then, come mid-October, a large, elaborate ancestor altar would be built, and offerings made. That was great, and something our whole household participated in.

Then I discovered that wasn't enough. My ancestor work deepened, and therefore, a larger altar—not the huge elaborate one, but one larger than the small one I used to have—needed a permanent place in my home.

We have an altar in the kitchen, where I leave a daily offering for our house spirit. When I make my cup of tea in the morning, I make one for the house spirit as well.

There is an offering stone in the garden, where libations get poured and offerings made. Our last home had a more manicured space, so we made offerings much more frequently. This current home, the backyard is more wild and less tamed. A friend immediately dubbed a central area "the fairy hollow."

We've found that, in listening to the land, the spirits don't want or need as many offerings. They're doing fine all on their own, and the gardening and yard work my one partner does is plenty. The water I leave out for the animals during the hot months and the food left out in winter is plenty.

Practice punctuates my family life. We express our gratitude and cultivate our relationships with beings seen and unseen in many ways.

When we center ourselves and pay attention, the world opens to our hearts and minds.

My hope is that practice will come to support every facet of your life and all of your relationships. My hope is that practice will enable us to live well and to be of service to this gorgeous world.

CLOSING AND OPENING

"Learn by practice." —Martha Graham

Take a moment now and breathe.

What is your current relationship to daily practice? What does that feel like?

On the days when you forgot or avoided it, what sort of energy levels, mental clarity, or emotional states arose throughout the day? Are you finding that, even on days when it feels like a fight to rise to your commitment, that the day starts even slightly more centered and connected to your deeper desires, or to spirit?

Spiritual practice not only helps all of our other endeavors, it gives us a sense of place in the cosmos. We are not alone in our striving. It is not just our egos that wish to make bread for our families, or take a walk beneath the trees with a friend, or feel moved by beautiful music. Our hearts and souls are engaged. Day by day, we become more fully activated and present to our lives, our Gods, the grace of Earth, and the glorious beauty of distant planets and stars.

Daily spiritual practice has also served to make me kinder and more compassionate, less harshly judgmental, and has helped shift my codependency to patterns of greater respect.

I'm still practicing.

There are still mornings where, ill slept, it may feel hard to get to the yoga mat or the meditation bench. But we can chart the results of both making the effort and not doing so.

Because of my years of observation of cause and effect, more often than not, I choose to return to practice. Occasionally I don't—taking a few breaths and sending out a simple prayer instead—and that's okay too.

Nothing is firm. Everything is a cycle, a process, a practice. Even practice itself.

I wish you success in the great unfolding of your life.

I wish you curiosity.

I wish you health.

I wish you the continued ability to return to center, and to practice every day.

Blessed be

ALSO BY T. THORN COYLE

NON-FICTION

Evolutionary Witchcraft

Kissing the Limitless

Make Magic of Your Life

Sigil Magic for Writers, Artists & Other Creatives

Crafting a Daily Practice

Resistance Matters

FICTION

Seashell Cove Paranormal Cozy Mysteries

Bookshop Witch

Haunted Witch

Tarot Witch

Running Witch

Hallows Witch

The Pride Street Paranormal Cozy Mysteries

Sushi Scandal

Flower Frenzy

Muffin Murder

The Witches of Portland (complete)

By Earth

By Flame

By Wind

By Sea

By Moon

By Sun

By Dusk

By Dark

By Witch's Mark

The Panther Chronicles (Complete)

To Raise a Clenched Fist to the Sky

To Wrest Our Bodies From the Fire

To Drown This Fury in the Sea

To Stand With Power on This Ground

The Steel Clan Saga

We Seek No Kings

We Heed No Laws

We Ride at Night

Short Story Collections

A Hint of Faery

A Touch of Faery

A Spark of Magic

A Flame for Yuletide

A Hope for Winter

A Time for Magic

A Speculation of Stars

A Speculation of Hope

A Speculation of Time

Risk It All: Queer Stories of Love, Suspense, And Daring

Thresholds: Queer Stories of Love, Suspense, And Daring

ABOUT THE AUTHOR

T. Thorn Coyle worked in many strange and diverse occupations before settling in to write novels. Thorn has been a student of the magical arts for forty years and taught in nine countries, on four continents, and in twenty-five states.

Author of the *Seashell Cove Paranormal Mystery* series, the *Pride Street Paranormal Cozy Mysteries*, *The Steel Clan Saga*, *The Witches of Portland*, and *The Panther Chronicles*, Thorn's multiple non-fiction books include *Sigil Magic for Writers, Artists & Other Creatives*, *Kissing the Limitless, Make Magic of Your Life,* and *Evolutionary Witchcraft.* Thorn's work also appears in many anthologies, magazines, and collections.

An interloper to the Pacific Northwest U.S., Thorn drinks a lot of tea, pays proper tribute to the neighborhood cats, and talks to crows, squirrels, and trees.

Connect with Thorn:
www.thorncoyle.com

www.ingramcontent.com/pod-product-compliance
Lightning Source LLC
Chambersburg PA
CBHW050323120526
44592CB00014B/2034